T0288714

# Ladders

## The
# Pueblo
## Pre-Columbian Americans

# WHO WERE THE ANCIENT PUEBLO?

by Nathan W. James

Buildings like the one in this photograph are some of the only evidence left to tell us about people who lived in what is now the southwestern United States more than 1,400 years ago. At first, the ancient Pueblo lived off the land. They moved from place to place. After a while, they began to build settlements in desert canyons. They also built homes hidden under cliffs.

The ancient Pueblo were clever builders. They were also skilled craftspeople and talented artists. We still do not know much of their story. Lucky for us, they left behind evidence like these buildings. These clues help us figure out who they were and how they lived.

The ruins of Cliff Palace near Cortez, Colorado, reveal how the ancient Pueblo built their homes.

## WHAT'S IN A NAME?

One mystery about the ancient Pueblo is what they called themselves. We only know what other tribes called them. The Navajo called them the Anasazi, which meant "ancient enemies." The Spanish called them the Pueblo, which is the Spanish word for "village." This name stuck. The ancient Pueblo are sometimes called ancestral Puebloans. That means they are the past relatives of today's Pueblo.

# WHERE FOUR CORNERS MEET

The ancient Pueblo lived in an area now known as the Four Corners. It is called the Four Corners because four states all meet at one point. These states are Colorado, New Mexico, Arizona, and Utah. Of course, there were no states thousands of years ago when the ancient Pueblo first lived here.

The Four Corners area has mountains and deserts. It also has rivers, such as the San Juan and the Colorado. The area has all kinds of weather. The mountains are chilly most of the year. The desert is hot and dry in the summer. Snow may be on the ground in some places during the winter.

The ancient Pueblo **migrated**, or moved, to the Four Corners area. They came from the west. Over time, most settled in the land we know today as southeastern Utah, southwestern Colorado, northeastern Arizona, and northwestern New Mexico.

Mountains tower over the desert lands and deep canyons of the Four Corners region.

# FOUR CORNERS REGION

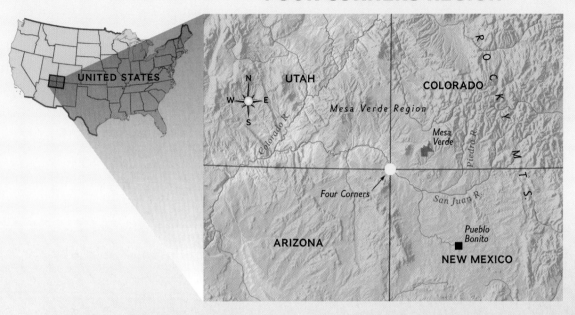

The Four Corners region includes the southern end of the Rocky Mountains and a portion of the Colorado River. It also includes Mesa Verde and several other ancient Pueblo sites. Read more about Mesa Verde later in this book.

# MYSTERIOUS ANCIENT PUEBLO

The ancient Pueblo did not leave a written history of their people. Luckily, the ruins of ancient Pueblo settlements are still in the Four Corners area. In northern New Mexico, **archaeologists** are figuring out the history of one of these settlements, Pueblo Bonito. Archaeologists are scientists who study past cultures. They are studying what is left of this settlement to learn about the ancient Pueblo.

Before living at Pueblo Bonito, the ancient Pueblo were **hunter-gatherers**. Hunter-gatherers hunted, fished, and picked nuts and berries to live. Around 1000 B.C., they began to farm. They grew crops such as corn, squash, and beans. Little by little, they began to build permanent homes in settlements. Pueblo Bonito was one of these settlements.

They began building Pueblo Bonito around A.D. 850. The building process went on for at least 200 years. The finished settlement was the shape of a capital D. It included more than 600 rooms. It was four to five stories tall. That's a tall structure compared to the desert around it.

The ancient Pueblo left Pueblo Bonito sometime during the 1200s. Why did they move away? Where did they go? Archaeologists still do not know. The ancient Pueblo may have migrated because of the weather. Or they may have needed to escape from enemies. Most archaeologists think they migrated to other parts of what is now New Mexico.

The end of Pueblo Bonito did not mean the end of the ancient Pueblo. As you continue reading, you'll learn about other amazing ancient Pueblo dwellings located in present-day southwestern Colorado.

This overhead view of Pueblo Bonito reveals its capital D shape.

The ancient Pueblo used the circles as homes. A roof made of straw covered each hole.

All of these circles make Pueblo Bonito look a little like a beehive.

They stored food and belongings in the square rooms.

The outer wall protected the settlement from its enemies. Anyone needing to enter or leave used a ladder, not a door.

# TODAY'S PUEBLO

More than 1,000 years have passed since Pueblo Bonito was built. The Pueblo people still live in the Four Corners area today.

The ancient Pueblo are the **ancestors**, or family members from long ago, of several modern Native American tribes. Some of these tribes are the Zuni, Rio Grande Pueblo, and Hopi. These tribes haven't moved very far from their ancestors' lands. The Rio Grande Pueblo are still in northern New Mexico. The Zuni settled at the border of New Mexico and Arizona.

The Hopi made northern Arizona their home. Some still live in traditional red clay houses like those in the community of Pueblo de Taos (shown below). Others live in cities such as Albuquerque (AL-buh-kur-kee), New Mexico.

Modern Pueblo people honor their ancient Pueblo ancestors by carrying on cultural traditions, or customs. One fun way they do this is by having a big party. Every year, the people of Pueblo de Taos host a

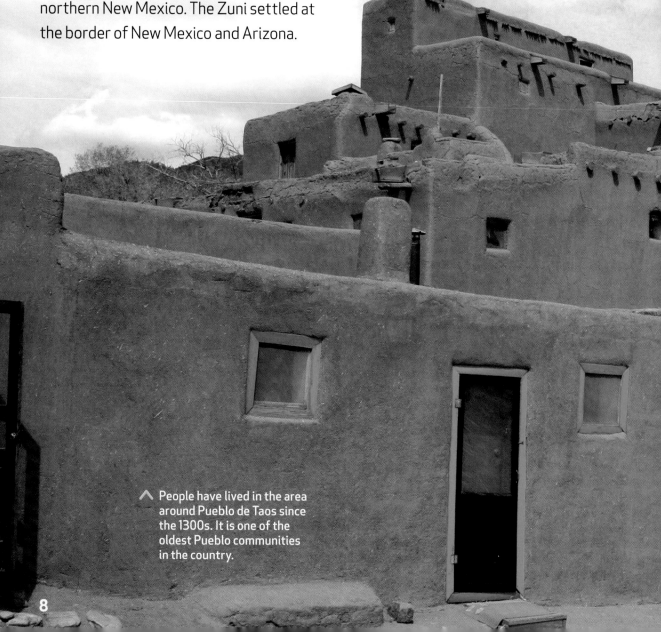

People have lived in the area around Pueblo de Taos since the 1300s. It is one of the oldest Pueblo communities in the country.

powwow. A powwow is a gathering of Native Americans to celebrate their cultures. At the powwow, people wear modern and traditional clothes. They dance and sing. They share foods such as corn, beans, and bread. These are some of the same foods the ancient Pueblo ate hundreds of years ago. During these parties, the modern world mixes with the ancient Pueblo world. It can feel as if only ten days, instead of a thousand years, have passed since the time of Pueblo Bonito.

Some modern Pueblo still bake bread in traditional adobe ovens called *hornos* (AWR-nohs).

In the past, people held powwows for many different reasons. At powwows, people gave thanks for good harvests, and warriors gathered courage before battles.

**Check In** Describe some of the ancient cultural traditions that modern Pueblo continue today.

# The Genius of the Ancient Pueblo

*by Brinda Gupta*

THE ANCIENT PUEBLO WERE A CLEVER PEOPLE. LET'S LOOK AT SOME OF THEIR INVENTIONS TO GET AN IDEA OF HOW THEY LIVED.

## Pithouses and Kivas

If you've ever visited the desert, you know how hot it is. The ancient Pueblo learned to get out of the sun. They dug buildings in the dirt to escape the heat.

One structure they built was a **pithouse**, a home inside of a pit. First, they dug a hole in the ground about three feet deep. Then they put wooden posts along the walls of the hole to support the roof.

They made roofs by spreading mud over sticks. When the mud dried, they cut two holes in the roof. One hole was for a ladder. That was the entrance. The other hole was to let out smoke from their fire. No one wants to live in a smoky house.

Ancient Pueblo builders dug even deeper into the ground for a different kind of building, called a **kiva**. This round building had a fireplace in the floor, usually in the center of the room. The ancient Pueblo used kivas mainly for religious events. They built spaces into the mud walls. They may have used these spaces to display special objects.

## PITHOUSE
Early pithouses usually had an entryway and a main chamber. The entryway had a ladder to the roof. It also had storage space for food and tools. The family lived in the main chamber. It was both a living room and a bedroom. The fireplace was in the center of the room.

∧ Many pithouses caught on fire. If a spark flew up, the dry stick roof would burn. The family would have to escape the pithouse quickly!

fire hearth
↓

← wall

∧ KIVA The long bench along the far wall of this rebuilt kiva provided seats for people. It also supported the walls and roof of the kiva.

< Kivas stayed cool all year-round. The cool temperatures there made them popular places to sleep.

# Tools and Weapons

Imagine eating dinner without a fork or digging a hole without a shovel. The ancient Pueblo did not have metal to make tools like these. They made tools out of materials they found, such as stones, feathers, and branches.

**∧ ARROWS** Some arrows have feathers on one end. This makes them spin in the air. The spinning makes the arrow go into its target. The ancient Pueblo made arrows from branches. Grooves in the wood held a stone arrowhead on one side and feathers on the other.

**> SPEARS** The ancient Pueblo sharpened stones by grinding them against a harder stone. They attached a sharpened stone to a long, straight branch to make a spear. They used spears to hunt. Have you ever seen an Olympic athlete throw a long spear called a javelin? That is how the ancient Pueblo threw their spears.

**ARROWHEADS** To make arrows, the ancient Pueblo shaped stones into sharp, pointed arrowheads. Then they attached the arrowheads to branches. To make bows, they soaked the wood in water and then bent it and let it dry. Twisted animal tendons provided string for the bows.

**AXES** An axe is made like a short spear, but the cutting stone is thicker. It has one or two sharp edges instead of a point at the tip. People used large axes to build kivas and pithouses. They used small axes to clear fields of brush.

**GRINDERS** The ancient Pueblo used two stones to grind corn. First, they poured the corn onto a long, flat stone called a *metate* (meh-TAH-tay). Then they pressed a smaller stone called a *mano* (MAH-no) onto the corn and rubbed the stone back and forth. Grinding the corn between the two rocks turned it into flour. They used this flour to make bread. They also used the stones to crush other foods for cooking.

13

# Baskets and Pottery

Long before they moved to the cliffs, the ancient Pueblo wove baskets. As their way of life changed from hunting to growing crops, they moved from place to place less often. Then they also began making pottery. Pottery was too heavy and fragile to take from place to place. When they settled in villages, pottery became more useful. Pots lasted longer than baskets and held more.

> **POTTERY DESIGNS** The ancient Pueblo decorated their pottery with patterns. Swirls were one kind of pattern they used. Pottery from the same area and time usually looks similar. Archaeologists look at the patterns of the pottery found at ancient Pueblo sites. The patterns give them clues to figure out when people lived there.

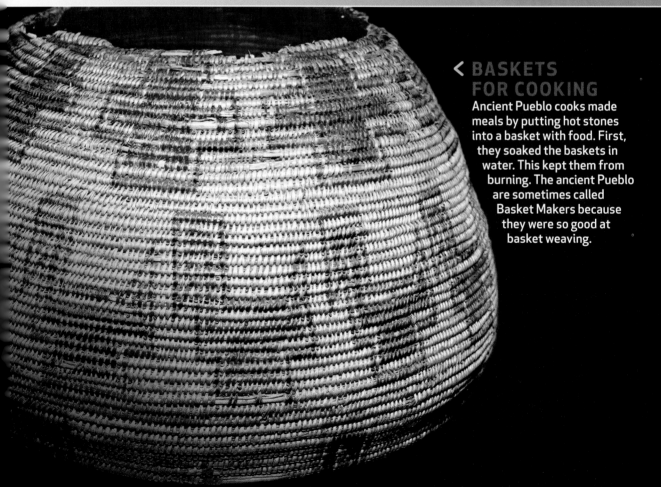

< **BASKETS FOR COOKING**
Ancient Pueblo cooks made meals by putting hot stones into a basket with food. First, they soaked the baskets in water. This kept them from burning. The ancient Pueblo are sometimes called Basket Makers because they were so good at basket weaving.

^ PITCHERS The ancient Pueblo crafted fine pottery, such as this pitcher shaped like a duck. They used pottery for storage containers, bowls, plates, mugs, and pots. Some pieces of pottery were made as art. They were created to look at, not to use.

∨ ARTS & CRAFTS

The way pottery is made hasn't changed much over time. Potters form shapes with clay and then harden the clay in an oven. The ancient Pueblo put the soft clay in pits near fires. Then they covered the pit, which turned it into a kind of oven. Once pottery hardens, artists decorate it. The ancient Pueblo used berries and other plants to make paint. Modern artists usually just buy paint.

# Maria Martinez

Maria Martinez was born in the 1880s. She spent her childhood in a small village outside of Santa Fe, New Mexico. The village was called San Ildefonso Pueblo. Almost everyone in her village traced their families back to the ancient Pueblo. Maria's aunt knew the ancient Pueblo ways of making pots. She taught these skills to Maria. Pueblo pottery became very popular in the early 1900s, when railroads brought white settlers to the area. They wanted to buy the beautiful pots.

Years later, archaeologists found ancient Pueblo pottery no one had seen before. The pottery was shiny black and decorated with a rough black pattern, as in the photo below. Maria wanted to copy this pottery using what she knew about the ancient Pueblo techniques.

After many tries, Maria was able to copy the black pottery style. Museums and art collectors began buying her pots. The new pots based on ancient artifacts drew people to Maria's studio. People became interested in southwestern Pueblo crafts. Maria lived into her 90s. Through her life, she taught her sons, grandchildren, and many others the art of making Pueblo pottery.

**Check In** What types of tools did the ancient Pueblo make?

> Cliff Palace hides under a ledge near Chapin Mesa. This mesa is located in the southern part of Mesa Verde National Park.

# Welcome to

**G**ood morning. Welcome to one of the most fascinating historical locations in the United States. This is Mesa Verde (MAY-suh VAIR-day) National Park in Cortez, Colorado. The park has ancient Pueblo ruins that date back to the 1200s. If you've never explored buildings built into cliffs before, then touring Mesa Verde will be an experience you'll never forget!

First, look at this **mesa**. A mesa is a flat, raised piece of land. See the small, dark openings in the rock? Those are the doorways and windows of houses the ancient Pueblo built into the rock. Your first stop, Cliff Palace, is the largest of the ancient Pueblo **dwellings**, or homes. It had 150 rooms. About 100 people lived there. It was sort of like a hotel or apartment building.

# Mesa Verde

*by Elizabeth Massie*

At first, the ancient Pueblo built their villages on top of the mesas. Then they began to build their homes into the steep cliff walls on the sides of the mesas. Putting their homes there solved two problems. First, the height of their homes made it harder for enemies to break in. Second, the cliff walls protected them from the harsh wind and sun of the desert.

Eventually, the ancient Pueblo **abandoned** Mesa Verde. It sat empty for hundreds of years. Around 1890, two brothers from a nearby ranch found the cliff dwellings while looking for their lost cows. They were amazed by what they found. Over the years, they visited Cliff Palace many times. They also convinced the U.S. government to make the area a national park. Thanks to those brothers, Al and Richard Wetherill, Mesa Verde will be kept safe and beautiful for many years.

The brick walls of Spruce Tree House kept the inside of the home warm on chilly winter days.

# Spruce Tree House

Your next stop is Spruce Tree House. This is the third largest cliff dwelling at Mesa Verde. It was one of the first buildings the Wetherill brothers found. Imagine how exciting it must have been to discover this ancient building instead of a stray cow.

Why is this dwelling called Spruce Tree House? It is because a large spruce tree once grew from the front of the home up to the top of the mesa. The first modern visitors to Spruce Tree House had to climb down the tree to get inside. But you won't have to climb down a tree to see this dwelling!

Spruce Tree House is huge. It has 130 rooms made of stone. Each of the rooms could fit 60 to 80 people. The people who lived there used the rooms for sleeping, visiting, and cooking.

There are eight kivas outside Spruce Tree House. We can climb down this ladder to look at one. A kiva is a small room dug into the ground. The ancient Pueblo used kivas for religious events and celebrations. The men of the village also met here to talk and make important decisions. The air stayed cool inside kivas year-round, so some people even slept in them on hot nights.

^ The fireplace and chimney are to the left of the ladder. The chimney helped to vent smoke out of this room in Spruce Tree House. The exit in the ceiling also helped keep the air inside from getting too smoky.

Most walls of Balcony House are still sturdy after hundreds of years of desert weather. The round hole you see in this photo is a kiva.

# Balcony House

Down the road from Cliff Palace and Spruce Tree House we'll begin the most adventurous part of your tour. Get ready! We'll be climbing a wide, steep ladder up to Balcony House.

When you reach the top of the ladder, check out the holes in the wall. When you spot what looks like a very low window, you've found the door. The ancient Pueblo built this cliff dwelling with defense in mind. Small, low doors were easy to close when the village was under attack. Also, the doors were tricks. To enemies, the small holes looked like windows.

Balcony House is smaller than the first two dwellings we visited. It has only 40 rooms. But the outdoor living areas are bigger. We will need to crawl through a 12-foot-long

Scared of heights? The ladder leading to Balcony House is 32 feet high.

tunnel to see it all. This house is built deep into the cliff. The flat rock that sticks out in front looks like a balcony. It gave the people who lived here a great view of the land below.

To leave Balcony House we will climb down another ladder and some stairs. It's hard work to visit homes built into the side of a cliff!

The first modern explorers of Mesa Verde found ancient pottery, discarded tools, and ash from fires in the rooms and kivas.

# Long House

Our last stop is in another part of Mesa Verde National Park. The Long House dwellings are in an area northwest of the other cliff dwellings. These homes are 130 feet high. They are under Wetherill Mesa.

Long House may have gotten its name from the very long house the ancient Pueblo built in the center of the cliff wall. As the community grew, the villagers added more rooms to the house. Like Balcony House, Long House is almost completely hidden beneath the cliffs. Security was important to the ancient Pueblo.

Long House is the second largest dwelling in Mesa Verde National Park. About 100 people lived in it. Look at the different rooms. Think about what living here would have been like. In some ways, the ancient Pueblo lived like we do. They built homes that kept them safe. They lived with their families. They spent a lot of time in their homes. There are differences, too. For example, you probably don't have to climb a ladder to enter your house.

It's time to end our tour of Mesa Verde National Park and the ancient Pueblo cliff dwellings. We hope that you learned new things about the people who once lived in these dwellings.

Wetherill Mesa

▽ This view shows how Wetherill Mesa protects Long House. The dwellings are hidden deep within the cliff walls.

Long House

**Check In** How do the sites at Mesa Verde help us to understand how the ancient Pueblo lived?

# ROCK ARTIST

by Erica Lauf

Meet Pueblo artist Jaque Fragua (JAKE FROW-wah). Jaque grew up in Jemez (HAY-muhs) Pueblo, New Mexico. Art and culture were around every corner. His interest in art started when he created his own clothing and jewelry. He made them to wear in traditional Pueblo dance performances. Now he travels the country painting and sharing his love of art with children.

"We wanted to make the wall dance." That's how Jaque explained why he and his friends created this 50-foot wall painting in Miami, Florida.

Hundreds of years ago, the ancient Pueblo created thousands of **petroglyphs** (PEH-truh-glifs), or rock carvings, such as the one shown below. They cut shapes into walls of volcanic rock. They used chisels and knives to cut the shapes into the rock. They chipped off the dark outer rock. This showed the light rock beneath. Many of these carvings can still be seen in the deserts of the Southwest. No one knows their exact meaning. They may have told a story, marked an event, or had a spiritual purpose. The artists made them very large and placed them where they couldn't be missed.

Today, Jaque follows in the footsteps of ancient Pueblo artists, but he makes his own wall painting with a modern twist. His main tool is spray paint. He paints on brick buildings, plywood walls, and billboards. His paintings splash across city landscapes.

Ancient people carved this petroglyph into a rock wall in New Mexico. Look to the left of center. There is a warrior holding a shield. The round shield is decorated with two bear claws.

# AN ARTIST AT WORK

Some people plan before they start a project. Jaque likes to jump right in. He doesn't use a sketch or a plan. He usually just grabs a spray can and starts making shapes. He makes very large paintings on buildings. This kind of surface or **canvas** is not always perfect. But a window can become an eye with a little spray paint.

Jaque shares his art with whole communities. He wants to bring people together to enjoy his art. He paints, dances, and writes poetry. He also blends these different art forms. He has even created art from garbage!

⌄ Jaque made the design on this garage door in San Francisco, California. He painted it to look like a fabric pattern.

⌃ This building in Albuquerque, New Mexico, was damaged by fire. Jaque turned it into a guardian watching over the neighborhood.

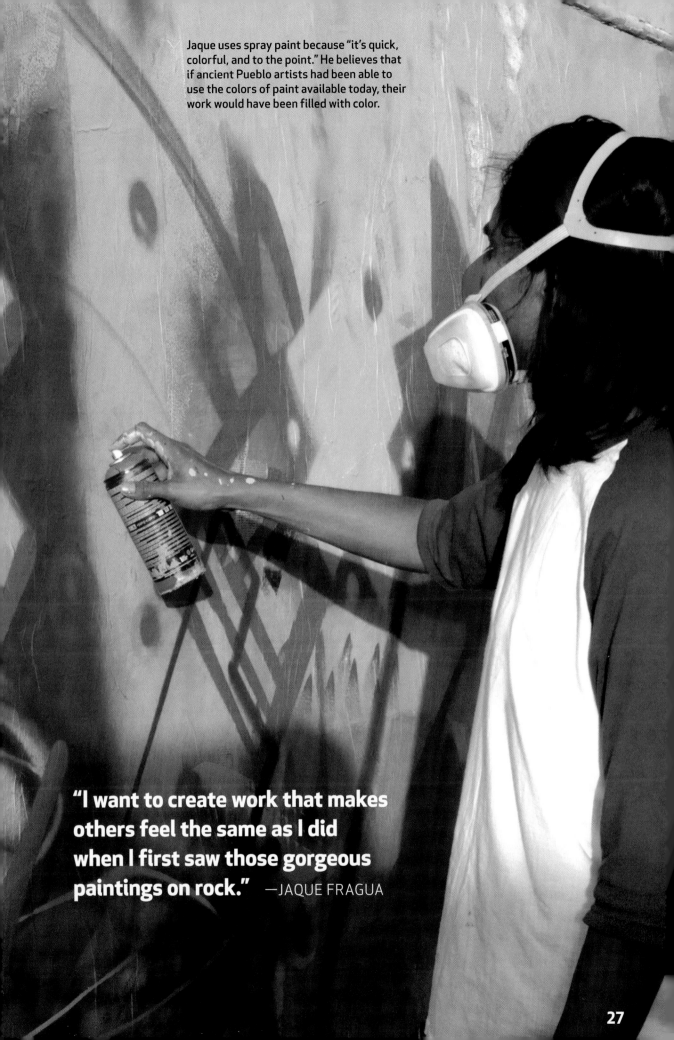

Jaque uses spray paint because "it's quick, colorful, and to the point." He believes that if ancient Pueblo artists had been able to use the colors of paint available today, their work would have been filled with color.

"I want to create work that makes others feel the same as I did when I first saw those gorgeous paintings on rock." —JAQUE FRAGUA

# IT'S IN THE DETAILS

Jaque worked on the **mural**, or wall painting, below in Miami, Florida. He painted it with a group of street artists known as the American Indian Mural Krew. He says the mural is meant to be a drawing of a prayer. The details of the painting may give you an idea of what the prayer is about.

The zigzag pattern in the picture below is a common design in Jaque's murals. This pattern could stand for lightning or energy. Look at the picture at the bottom of the page. There are two rounded shapes to the left of Jaque. One shape is bright yellow and orange. The other is mostly white with blue and pink lines. Some people might think these shapes look like feathers.

⌄ Look at this zigzag pattern. What does the pattern make you think about?

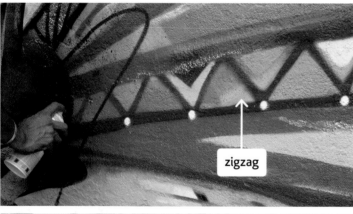

zigzag

feathers

⌃ Feathers are common Pueblo symbols. They usually stand for prayer. This makes sense when you remember Jaque described this mural as a painted prayer.

A pattern at the top of this building looks like tilted stairways.

bird

feathers

fish

# TEACHING OTHERS

Jaque also spends time helping others make art. The way he paints on his own is different from the way he paints with others.

Teaching art to children is important to Jaque. Painting and teaching are two ways he shares his Pueblo identity. He explains, "Art is a way to connect generations. We have a great past to learn from, but there is also a bright future."

Jaque helped students make this mural in Pawhuska, Oklahoma. First, they created the design on a computer. Then Jaque used a projector to shine the design onto the wall. He sketched the outline of the mural with spray paint. Finally, the students filled in the designs with colors.

Jaque sees art as a way to bring people together. This young volunteer uses a paintbrush to touch up part of the mural. With many hands helping, the team painted this mural in just a few days.

This student uses a roller to help paint the background. Jaque says, "I put great priority (importance) on traveling and creating work in places all over the world. I think it's the only way we can truly learn to grow—by firsthand experience."

Check In | Why does Jaque Fragua think art is important?

## Discuss

1.  What connections can you make among the four selections in the book? How are the selections related?

2.  How have the land and environment influenced the ways both the ancient and modern Pueblo have lived?

3.  The third selection gives us information about the ancient Pueblo. Use the text to explain how archaeologists use evidence from the ruins to understand this ancient culture.

4.  In what ways does Jaque Fragua borrow ideas and designs from the ancient Pueblo petroglyphs?

5.  What are some mysteries that remain about the ancient Pueblo? What else would you like to know about them?